Rasha Faraj

E-tourism Revolutionary Effect

Studying E-tourism in Lebanon

LAP LAMBERT Academic Publishing

Impressum / Imprint

Bibliografische Information der Deutschen Nationalbibliothek: Die Deutsche Nationalbibliothek verzeichnet diese Publikation in der Deutschen Nationalbibliografie; detaillierte bibliografische Daten sind im Internet über http://dnb.d-nb.de abrufbar.

Alle in diesem Buch genannten Marken und Produktnamen unterliegen warenzeichen-, marken- oder patentrechtlichem Schutz bzw. sind Warenzeichen oder eingetragene Warenzeichen der jeweiligen Inhaber. Die Wiedergabe von Marken, Produktnamen, Gebrauchsnamen, Handelsnamen, Warenbezeichnungen u.s.w. in diesem Werk berechtigt auch ohne besondere Kennzeichnung nicht zu der Annahme, dass solche Namen im Sinne der Warenzeichen- und Markenschutzgesetzgebung als frei zu betrachten wären und daher von jedermann benutzt werden dürften.

Bibliographic information published by the Deutsche Nationalbibliothek: The Deutsche Nationalbibliothek lists this publication in the Deutsche Nationalbibliografie; detailed bibliographic data are available in the Internet at http://dnb.d-nb.de.

Any brand names and product names mentioned in this book are subject to trademark, brand or patent protection and are trademarks or registered trademarks of their respective holders. The use of brand names, product names, common names, trade names, product descriptions etc. even without a particular marking in this works is in no way to be construed to mean that such names may be regarded as unrestricted in respect of trademark and brand protection legislation and could thus be used by anyone.

Coverbild / Cover image: www.ingimage.com

Verlag / Publisher:
LAP LAMBERT Academic Publishing
ist ein Imprint der / is a trademark of
OmniScriptum GmbH & Co. KG
Heinrich-Böcking-Str. 6-8, 66121 Saarbrücken, Deutschland / Germany
Email: info@lap-publishing.com

Herstellung: siehe letzte Seite /
Printed at: see last page
ISBN: 978-3-659-52504-9

Copyright © 2014 OmniScriptum GmbH & Co. KG
Alle Rechte vorbehalten. / All rights reserved. Saarbrücken 2014

Rasha Faraj

E-tourism Revolutionary Effect

<u>Acknowledgement</u>

First of all, I would like to say Alhamdulillah, for giving me the strength and health to do this project work until it was done.

I am heartily thankful to my supervisor; Head of the Travel & Tourism department, Prof. Hussein Chible, whose encouragement, guidance and support from the initial to the final level enabled me to develop an understanding of the subject.

Special thanks would go to our Dean, Prof. Kamal Hammad, for always being there for me when I needed him the most.

Lastly, I offer my regards and blessings to all of those who supported me in any respect during the completion of the project.

<u>Dedication</u>

To my family, who have always been there for me, and have never doubted my dreams.

For a very precious...Who gave me time which was the most valuable gift for me.

To all that find contentment within its pages.

To the authors of the hundreds of books and research articles, without which there would be nothing to support my words, I give you praise

Abstract

E-tourism has shown effective influence on tourism development with all its kinds through its implementation. It has facilitated the job of tourism stakeholders yet showed negative impacts. The purpose of this study is to show how tourism been affected by the revolution of ICT and what are the negatives and positive of e-tourism and how to manage and develop it taking Lebanon as an area to study on. The results showed that even though the negatives occur, however development must be done and evolution of the internet will help both consumers and producers in attaining their targets.

Keywords: E-tourism, ICT, Management, Website, Virtual Tourism.

Table of Contents

Chapter 1: Introduction

1.1 General View

Tourism has become mostly the biggest industry in the world. It is an export industry that brings hard money for the country and many countries are counting on this sector for the development of their economy.

Internet has become an intermediary in every single step of our lives. It is the new solution for everything. It has improved and developed tourism in which has swiped tourism to an E-tourism or electronic tourism.

It is one of the fastest developing technologies. It involves the consumer and the provider of tourism but in a new concept. The provider has become directly to the internet. Those providers are the partners or components of the tourism industry itself like travel agencies, tour operators, airlines, hotels, car rentals…

E-tourism offers the consumer lots of services that he is requesting and by doing them online without any intermediary for help. The consumer can take information, do bookings, request services, ask for help, increase his knowledge, buy and sell, all these can be done through the internet. This developed tourism and turned this industry from a developing to more technological one.

1.2 Purpose of the Study

This thesis is going to focus on better understanding the concept of e-tourism, and how it is affecting the tourism sector and where it stands now and in the future, so the problems that will be discussed here are:

➢ Why E-tourism is important? And what are its advantages and disadvantages?

➢ What are the ways to develop E-tourism?

1.3 Methodology

This thesis will be done by returning to some books and scientific articles related to electronic tourism or e-business, making interviews with some agencies and hotels in Lebanon, distributing questionnaires on travel and tourism companies in order to get more information about the effect of internet on their revenues during the last five years.

1.4 Outline of the Study

Many Chapters have been discussed in this project:

Chapter 2 will show different examples about development of e-tourism in some countries in order to show where it was and how it has been developed, and also some important tourism websites that are very effective for reservation and how they reached this high level for applying reservations.

Chapter 3 will include the definition of e-tourism, its history, where it was, how it developed and e-tourism in the future. The following points will be discussed in details:

• E-tourism Definition.

- E-tourism History
- Types of websites developed
- E-tourism and the Future.
- E-tourism in Lebanon.

Chapter 4 will include all the interviews that I have made and all the questionnaires distributed either on customers or on travel agencies with their statistics and final results concerning e-tourism development in Lebanon.

Chapter 5 will discuss how e-tourism has affected on companies either positively or negatively. The following points will be discussed in details:

- Benefits of E-commerce
- E-tourism positives and negatives
- Management and development of e-tourism in Lebanon.

Chapter 6 will include many steps on how to make the website easier for the customer in order to attain his reservation without anything getting wrong as much as it would be.

Chapter 7 will show a website "created by me" about Lebanon Underwater, all the information about underwater ruins with their photos and videos. This chapter includes:

- History.
- Why virtual Tour
- Virtual tourism of Lebanon underwater through a website
- SWOT analysis of the website
- Conclusion

Chapter 8 will present the ways in order to make e-tourism more applicable in Lebanon are discussed in here and studying the marketing mix in Lebanon.

In order to begin with the project, I had to see some examples of the effect of internet on the travel and tourism companies, and so on the next chapter, many case studies have been inserted to give an idea about e-tourism's effect on many different countries around the world and to get some information from these case studies and apply them on our agencies in Lebanon.

Chapter 2: Case Studies

This chapter includes four case studies showing where E-tourism is in some countries or even important travel websites, how are they affecting on the plans of tourists for travelling and taking some of these ideas and applying them in Lebanon.

2.1 Case 1: E-tourism in England

E-tourism in England has been taken as a strategy for developing tourism there through ICT and e-business.

After a study done on UK homes, it has been shown that around 50% of the populations use the internet and the biggest product of all is travel and tourism, in which the usage of the internet is for taking information and buying tickets. They also use emails in order to reach customers more, and improve their marketing. So, there is a strong relationship between the internet and tourism industry as a whole.

According to statistics made by Britain, internet usage has increased by the end of 2001, yet this growth is increasing day by day and many technologies have been improved to be used in the future.

The reason of using internet is to get information from home. However, difficulties occurred in the UK, since consumers had problems of website usability, incomplete bookings, and consumer concerns of security in payments or price difference.

Moreover, big companies created websites to allow consumers to make reservations online, in which it has created obstacles for small and medium enterprises to do the same as big ones. They do not have pro-active actions to move towards e-business

So, in order to avoid these difficulties, e-tourism strategies had been considered to develop and promote e-tourism in England.

Summary

Nobody really knows just how many people in the UK and around the world are now using the Internet. One thing that is clear, however, is that the Internet has revolutionized the way the world works, and the tourism industry has to adapt to the emerging 'digital economy' in a big way.

2.2 Case 2: Omni Tourism

It is an important website for travel and tourism. It is one of the important successful websites because of its focus in building sustainable relations between consumers and producers through providing easy access and offering different services.

Figure 1: What information Omni offers

Since 2000, different leaders contributed in development of Omni website. This website helps suppliers and consumers and offers not only reservations, information, and services, but only consultation. It is the most sustainable development strategy applied to improve e-tourism worldwide.

2.3 Case 3: E-tourism in Vietnam

The E-commerce is at its beginning in Vietnam. The problem of the internet usage in Vietnam is mainly for documentation and communication. Tourism wasn't their focus, only few websites look for tourism in Vietnam related to accommodation.

It is vital to develop tourism in Vietnam by improving electronic tourism through the help of the Tourism Information Technology Center (TITC).

The job of the TITC is to develop the Tourism information system in Vietnam and offer services and information for consumers of the tourism and hospitality field.

Only 4 websites are interested and focused on tourism. The job of TITC is to make tests on new websites to develop them and allow reservation online.

2.4 Case 4: Trip advisor Website

By 2010, TripAdvisor was the largest travel site in the world operating in 24 countries and 16 languages, it assists its customers with review about destinations, hotels, and services that have been faced by people all over the world. It was founded in February 2000 by Stephen Kaufer.

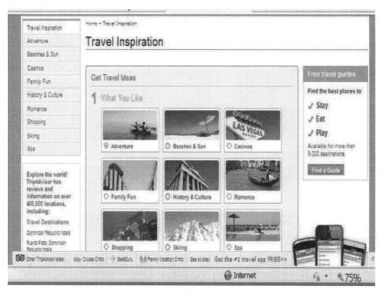

Figure 2: travel ideas that Tripadvisor offers to its customers

What tripadvisor faces is that whether the critics left from customers about the attractions/hotels they have visited are true or not.

Moreover, tripadvisor cannot lose its customer confidence, so that's why tripadvisor say that they use a system that the reader use a variety of cues to see whether he can take the review into account or not. Also, it is mentioned that the commenter should leave information about himself in order to increase information confidence.

However, leaving comments is not an easy way. Commenters should be encouraged to leave their comments and thoughts. This is a problem by itself.

Summary

It turns out that there is more than making reservations or making virtual tours by using the internet in general and Tripadvisor specifically, visitors can get more information about any hotel or a location they are thinking of getting to that they can through other visitor's opinions built their own thoughts about what to do during their trip.

2.5 Conclusion

Finally, after studying many case studies, it seems that electronic tourism has become more and more important as the internet is spread, so we should take a closer look on this type of tourism and try to find ways to develop it.

In the next chapter, e-tourism will be defined, its history and its future with the development of its websites through the past years, so let's have a look on it.

Chapter 3: E-tourism Revolution

This chapter will define e-tourism, its history on how it started and its future, and what are the types of websites that have been reached until now.

3.1 E-tourism Definition

Buhalis (2003) suggests that e-tourism reflects the digitization of all processes and value chains in the tourism, travel, hospitality and catering industries.

It includes e-commerce and all the information communication technologies that build a revolution for all business. E-tourism affects positively and facilitates the work of tourism organizations and improves their working process.

E-business is the biggest one of all. E-commerce, e-tourism, and e-marketing are sub-segments of e-business. The 3 together build a successful organization. E-commerce helps the tourism sector through the ICT innovation. This helps in economic development and new step upwards for the tourism industry to move from a practical level to technological one that will boost tourism more and more and helps globally passing the services that tourism sector offers to all people around the world.

E-tourism includes all the electronic strategies, marketing, commerce, human resources, planning and development and management. So, in conclusion, it turns out that E-tourism describes a new way of doing business.

3.2 E-tourism History

It has been said that The Internet is the most important innovation since the development of the printing press.

When the internet started to appear, purchasing was the most requested service done by using the internet. Moreover, travel and tourism services were part of this purchase, they helped website visitors to buy, see, conduct information, leave a comment, and interact effectively to achieve the best buying offers.

Tourism and ICTs are related together and integrated in a way that cannot be apart. At the beginning of reservations, many reservation systems occurred to facilitate the work of travel agents and airlines and ensure easiness of work between companies all together. As an example, at first, it has been known that any customer wants to travel; he should have issued a paper ticket of about 20 pages that he has to take with him at the airport in order to hop-up on the airplane. However, at the beginning of 2000, paper tickets were changed into electronic tickets, only a small carton can take the customer to the destination he wants. Moreover, nowadays, there is no need to even have a ticket, it is enough to know at what time is your travel departure, and just go to the airport and fly. E-tourism has been developed dramatically in no time, all this development is related to ICT. It has changed tourism to the best for it is helping in building relations between tourism and its distribution channels.

As it will be seen in the market study chapter, most airlines have moved from Computer reservation systems to systems connected to the internet, user-friendly, and less time consuming.

3.3 Development Types of Websites

3.3.1 Web 1.0

It is the beginning of website development. It is the age of "reading, receiving, and responding". Web 1.0 is a read only web. Customers can search and take information but no interaction is allowed, focuses mainly on companies.

3.3.2 Web 2.0

It is the second generation website. Here, visitors can take and give information. Interaction exists here. It is a read-write web, includes Blogs, tagging…its concept is about sharing information that focuses on communities.

3.3.3 Web 3.0

It is the semantic web. You can speak and take the information directly, no need to wait for replying with no borders to face. It is the portable personal web, like mobile webs…

As a summary, we can say that in web 1, the relation is direct, the producer gives the information and the consumer receives it on the other side. For web 2, the producer gives information, the consumer receives it and also another producer might give information at the same time. However, in web3, many producers give information connected together, reached by the consumer.

3.4 E-tourism Prospects

The internet has become now a way of life. It is a new shuffle for living. Without the internet, people might be lost, don't know what to do if the internet disappeared for 5 minutes. It has become an addiction yet reality and fact that without the internet, we cannot reach out targets and more loss of time will be handled. E-tourism is now the future of the tourism industry as a whole, hotels, accommodation, restaurants, car rental, airlines… it is not just making reservations online in which having less time to reach what we want, but also the internet can help through virtual tours to know about destinations worldwide and gain knowledge and have experience within his/her home stay.

Even though E-tourism is the main reach for the future, however it is very important to ensure and build trust for customers to buy services through the internet. This cannot be done easily especially in Lebanon, cause people and specifically baby boomers are not ready till the moment to buy online. They believe that whenever they are going to buy through their credit cards, stealing will be a true grasp for them.

Ensuring customer loyalty and building trust and security are the main problem e-tourism would face. So, it is vital to show that this fear is nothing but just an idea drawn in our minds not more. There should be trust on both sides, not only from the company that owns the website, but also from the customer who is buying from it, it is a vice versa relation.

3.5 E-tourism In Lebanon

In Lebanon, we can notice that day after day the Lebanese travel agencies are becoming more aware and depending on the internet in all the fields including the tourism and hospitality. As a result of the diffusion of the internet, the travel agencies, tour operators and hotels created websites that allow users to check different packages and make reservations online by their own without needing any help from agent.

Statistics show that an important share of the work of the Lebanese travel agencies is made online and the proof is that the most important Lebanese travel agencies created "Internet Travel Agencies" like Kurban travel which created UFlyOnline.com and Nakhal who created hoojoozat.com. Both, Kurban and Nakhal hired specified staff to receive and interpret the bookings which showed the big load of bookings made online. Moreover, other agencies are turning now into online reservation systems such as Lena Tours, Anastasia Travel and Rida Travel.

As for the Lebanese hotel business, a significant number of their bookings come from international internet agencies such as Gulliver's travel, Destination of the WORLD, Booking.com and Tourico Holidays Travel agencies. The European and American markets book their rooms through GDS using the credit card paying method.

In the Globalization era, E-tourism is becoming the ultimate way to plan, book and promote all types of tourism and all destinations.

3.6 Conclusion

Finally, we can see that E-tourism is on continuous development from all its levels since the 1970's, and this development has been very successful. And also in Lebanon, we have seen where E-tourism is now, so we are going to see in the next chapter the effect of E-tourism, its advantages and disadvantages.

In the next chapter, market analysis is done for getting extra information about e-tourism development in Lebanon.

Chapter 4: Market Analysis

This chapter includes four interviews that are related to my project and two questionnaires. One of the questionnaires was distributed on the Lebanese people and the other were questions answered by agencies and tour operators. These questionnaires and interviews were made to see where e-tourism is now and what might happen in the future.

The questionnaire is quantitative, and the interviews are more qualitative.

4.1 Interviews

4.1.1 First Interview: At Movenpick

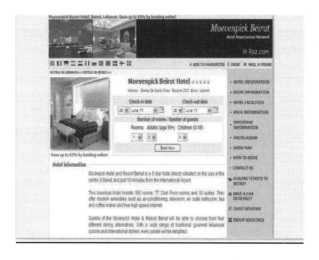

Figure 3: Movenpick hotel website

An interview was made in Movenpick with the reservation department on 7 April 2011. (Figure 3shows the homepage of the Movenpick).Several Questions were asked which were:

- Have customers used your website for reservation?

- Have revenues increased after creating the website?

- Are the prices on the website the same or less than the usual?

- Would the development of your website affected on the number of employees?

The reservation department employees gave me some information not much (because of the hotel's security) but helped me a little bit. The answers were that customers have increased after making their website. And as a result, as customers increase, revenues also increased.

Now, according to prices offered on the website, they are the same most of the time like when making reservation through an agent or directly with the hotel, however, sometimes they do put lower prices than the regular ones for promotion.

Finally, according to the number of employees, that when a website is made, people think that internal customers will decrease but it turned out to be not true and sometimes employee numbers might increase because the hotel needs more people following the website and making updates on it from time to time.

One extra thing I have noticed after seeing their website, they have a "Guest review" that allows their guests to leave their comments and ideas about their experience that they have faced during their stay, and this is truly a very important idea that gives hints for other customers about what they might face if they are going to stay in it.

4.1.2 Second Interview: At Phoenicia Hotel

On 23 of June 2011, this interview has been made for having more information on where E-tourism has reached in Lebanon, and Phoenicia was my target. (Figure 13 shows Phoenicia hotel Homepage website).

This interview could be done without the help of Mr. Georges Saaiby, Madame Maya Hanna (PR Department) and Mr. Rami Hamzi (Reservation Department), through them I took all the information that I am going to submit.

Phoenicia Hotel was part of intercontinental resorts and hotels around the world. Now, it is trying to leave the older standards and making their own ones.

Most of its customers are from the Gulf area, when they come to Lebanon, they go to Phoenicia hotel and if someone tells them to go to intercontinental they won't know it, they just know that it is Phoenicia. That's why they are trying to make their new steps in developing their name "Phoenicia" without intercontinental.

Figure 4: main Phoenicia website

Mostly, the most important way to make reservation is through a system called "Holidex", it is a computer reservation system (CRS) which allows its employees to do reservation easily and fast.

According to reservation through the internet, they used to have the website of Intercontinental, but now they are building their own site which is: http://www.phoeniciabeirut.com/. This site is still under construction. However, you can go to this site and you will see a slide show of the hotel, in and out, its location, and some attractions in Lebanon that could really help tourists informing them about tourism in Lebanon.

I noticed that the color of the website is Purple, when I asked why,, Mrs. Hanna told me that purple is the color of royalty,, the color which is associated with nobility. This color is put because of their respect and appreciation to their customers and how they make them feel as if they are treated like royalty during their stay in their hotel.

For booking through this site, since the site hasn't been finished yet, you will find on the right side of the site a "reservations", click on it and will take you to the intercontinental site, there you can make your reservation.

Figure 5: after clicking on reservation, it will take you to the Intercontinental website

4.1.3 Third Interview: at the Ministry Of Tourism

Also an interview I have made on 7/7/2011 with Mr. Joseph Farah, the consultant of Minister Fadi Abboud.

Figure 6: Ministry of Tourism Homepage

However, when I went there, when I asked about getting more information about e-tourism, they told me that they haven't yet made any researches about this type of tourism especially in the statistics and research department and that I should go to the ministry of telecommunication for more help on my topic. I mentioned this interview even though I did not get any help from them but still they tried to help me on getting a meeting with someone responsible at the telecommunication ministry.

4.1.4 Fourth Interview: with Air France

An interview was made on 14th of July at Air France with Mr. Joseph Daou (manager) and Madame Tuline Fares (supervisor).

At Air France, they used to have a CRS which is Amadeus, a lot of entries to be made for making a reservation, penalties, revalidation and many more. However, now they have changed their system to a new one called OSCAR, which they can login to it through the internet and make reservation from any place they want through of course a password.

This OSCAR is very easy to use, a lot of entries are now unneeded and a lot of time consuming is vanished because of the easy access and faster reservation making.

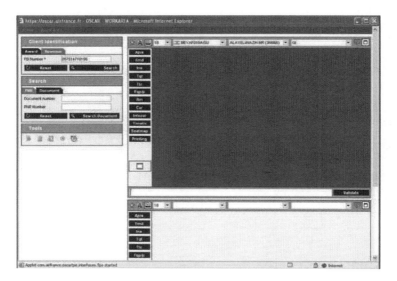

Figure 7: OSCAR System at Air France airlines

As we can see, under client identification, you can now just put the file number of the customer to open his reservation, unlike what they used to do in order to open a file they should take the customer's family name, date and time of travel and the flight number to just open it, imagine how much it would take time to take these information for just opening a file, now with just one click, the file opens and the agent can do anything the customer requests him to do.

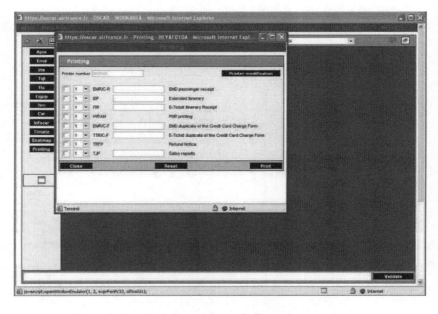

Figure 8: For obtaining a ticket, printing, sales reports

Another example, for obtaining a sales report, ticket,MCO… only one click on a key named "Printing", it will give you any choice you pick and just click "print" and all what you ask for will be done without wasting anytime.

4.2 Questionnaires

4.2.1 First Questionnaire (distributed on customers)

This questionnaire has been distributed on different people (75) to know whether they have used internet in Lebanon for reservation purposes or not, and why they have chosen this type? And for what?

After analyzing the answers, these charts were made to explain in more details what those people have answered.

The most of the persons who filled my questionnaire were between 18-25 years old with a percentage of 60%, and the other 40% are from 26years old and above.

The people who filled this questionnaire were of sexes, males and females.

The Questions that were analyzed are what follows on the next pages.

1. *Do you know about E-tourism?*

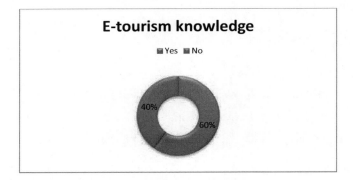

Referring to the chart above, 60% of customers have complete knowledge about e-tourism. However, the other 40% of customers have no idea about this type of tourism.

2. *Have you ever used any website related to reservations and booking?*

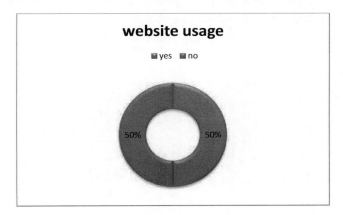

Referring to the chart above, it turns out that 50% of customers have referred to website usage for reservations and booking, while the other 50% haven't. Those 50% of them, almost about 30% are those who haven't known about this type of tourism.

3. *How many times have you done it?*

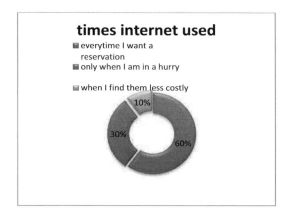

Referring to the above chart, 60%make their reservation on the internet when they need it, 10% when the reservations are found less costly when reserving through a website and 30% when they are in a hurry.

4. *Why do you use the internet rather than going to an agency or tour operator?*

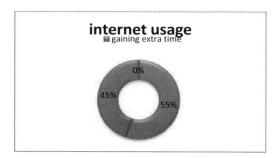

Referring to the above chart, 45% use the internet for their fewer prices; on the other hand, 55% use the internet in order to gain some extra time.

5. *What services related to your trip do you purchase online?*

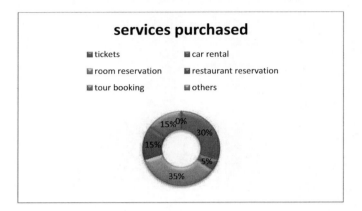

Referring to the above chart, from the internet, there are 35% who purchase room reservations,30% usually purchase tickets,15% purchase tour booking, but there are 15% that may also purchase restaurant reservations, and 5% purchase for car rentals

6. *Would E-tourism in Lebanon increases tourism cash flow?*

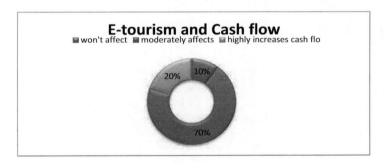

70% believe that e-tourism would moderately affect the cash flow in Lebanon, 20% believe that e-tourism would highly increase cash flow in Lebanon, and 10% believe that it has no effect at all.

7. *Do you think that the ministry of tourism should promote E-tourism in Lebanon?*

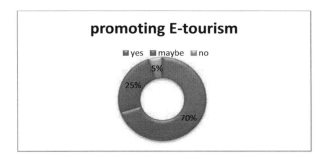

Referring to the chart above, 70% believe that the ministry of tourism app for promoting e-tourism in Lebanon, 25% thinks that it could promote this type of tourism in Lebanon. However, 5% believe that it won't.

8. *Do you think that the private sector should promote e-tourism in Lebanon?*

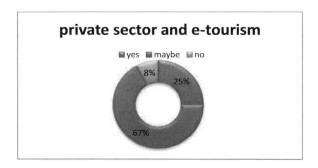

Referring to the results above, it seems like 67% believe that the idea for private sector in promoting the e-tourism in Lebanon might be a good way. May also, about 25% suppose that e-tourism should be promoted through the private sector, yet there are 8% that do not support this type of promotion.

9. *What are the ways for promoting E-tourism in Lebanon?*

Referring to the figure above, 52% support the usage of TAs, hotels, and car rentals for promoting e-tourism. 41% on the other hand support the usage of TV, Facebook, and advertising. There is also 7% that usually refer to ambassadors.

10. *Do you think that the ministry of telecommunication in Lebanon would have an effect on E-tourism?*

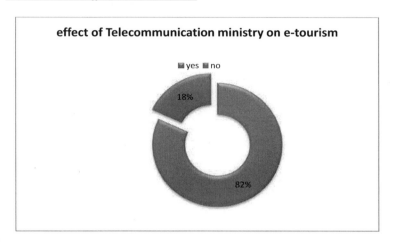

Based on the chart above, 82% believe that the telecommunication ministry will have an effect on e-tourism in Lebanon because of its direct connectivity with it.18% on the other, don't agree.

11. *What do you think about the product you are getting from the internet would be?*

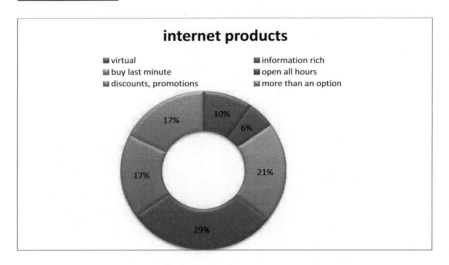

According to the above chart, 29% like to make their reservations through the internet because it is open all hours, 21% use it for the last minute, 17% use the net for getting more choices when doing their reservations, 17% have chosen promotions and discounts as a way for using the internet, while 10% believe that internet products are virtual and 6% say that the internet delivers an information rich for its customers.

12. *Finally, do you think that E-tourism would succeed in Lebanon?*

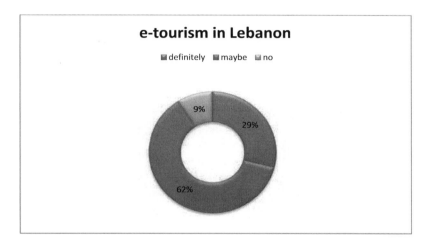

More than 60% of the people believe that e-tourism would have a chance to succeed in Lebanon, for 29% assure its succession with 9% who believe that this type of tourism has no future in Lebanon because of the bad telecommunication services offered these days.

As a result, we can conclude that e-tourism in Lebanon is on its way to become more and more developed and that it can be more applicable when it became known by its Lebanese customers with the encouragement and support of the tourism and telecommunication ministries.

6 questions were been asked on 15 travel agencies in order to see if they are using the internet for reservations or not and if they have created their own websites and would it be helpful for them in order to bring more customers.

These questions are at the end of this project (in appendix B).

8 of 15 travel agencies said that they have created their own websites while 7 said that they do not have a website. However, 3 of the TAs who answered no said that they are going to have their websites in the near future.

Out of 8 Travel agencies, 5 said that they are using their websites because it makes the work easier for them, 2 said that it has increased their sales and 1 said that it has increased their number of customers.

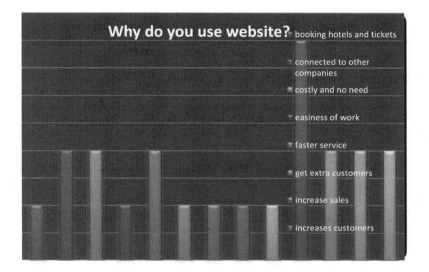

This chart was done after asking another 15 agencies in order to get more information on why they are using websites. As we can see before, we got only three reasons for using a website but on this chart the reasons increased and became more open.

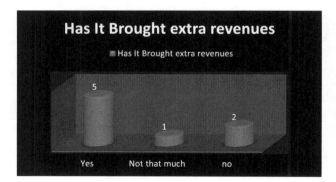

More than half of TAs that have a website said that it has brought for them more revenues, 1 said that it wasn't that much and 2 said that it hasn't increased their revenues at all.

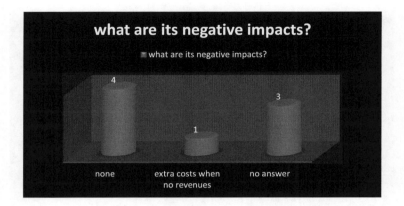

4 out of 8 said that it has no negative impacts and 3 did not gave an answer while 1 agency said that it is considered as an extra cost when there are no revenues to bring from.

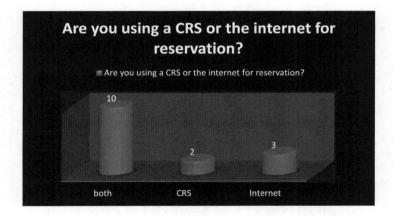

10 out of 15 agencies said that they are now using both the internet and CRS for making their reservations. 2 agencies are still using only CRS for reservations while 3 agencies are using the internet only for

their work and they said that it is accomplishing what they want to make.

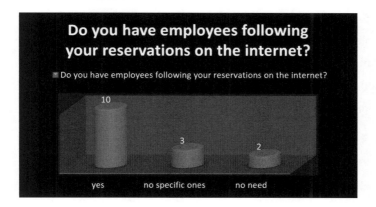

More than half of the agencies have put employees for making reservations online while only 2 agencies said that there is no need to put employees specialized on making reservations online.

As a conclusion, Travel agencies are becoming more and more moving towards the e-business formula and most of their businesses have become easier when using the internet during their reservations. Yet, those TAs that are not using the internet until now, they are going to in the near future because of the extra competitiveness they are facing with TAs that are using the internet and with the booking websites online.

In the next chapter, the effect of e-tourism will discussed with all its advantages and disadvantages, and how to manage it. So let's see what they are in chapter 5.

Chapter 5: E-tourism Effect & Management

Different benefits have been revealed for the development of E-tourism. There has been a shift from manual to digital use of mostly everything in our lives, yet we cannot say that technology haven't developed and improved the way of living even though it might have some negatives. So, in this chapter, we are going to see how E-tourism can affect positively or negatively on daily basis activities.

5.1 Positives of E-tourism

E-tourism has facilitated the work of travel agents, airlines, hotels, and customers who are able to interact directly with the company from home and make their service by themselves according to their priorities and preferences. E-tourism has offered lots of positives in which they include:

- It is an open business.

- Easy customer service.

- Great prices, if not as if you want to take it from the company, it could be at even lower price.

- Information reaches directly to customer.

- No time consuming.

- Can see all types of products and choosing the most applicable one.

- Let's consumers interact with other consumers (leaving comments, discussions…)

- Discover cities at home.

- Customers can do check-in before arriving to the hotel, to reduce congestion.

- Internet reaches all people, focuses on none, and targets all.

5.2 Negatives of E-tourism

As been said before, everything has its positives and negatives, wherever science will reach, still negative impacts will exist. E-tourism, with all its positives, still has some negatives in which will be mentioned as follows:

- Information not always right.

- Travel agents will reach a time where they will not find any role for them in the market. Internet will fill their jobs.

- Safety and security levels are still a controversial issue. This leads to no trust in the trade and commerce through the internet.

- Some people still feel safe when they go to the agency, see the agent, take the service or product and leave.

- No standards taken into account when posting the services and information.

- Big companies won't face the problems of small ones. Small companies won't be able to compete with the big or global ones, and this will lead to their closure.

- Creating software to build a high technology costs a lot, little companies can afford it.

With all the negatives, communities should walk with innovation and improvement. E-tourism is the revolution of the tourism industry, it is the destination that all are looking for; yet negatives can be avoided with good management.

5.3 Management & Development of E-tourism

To manage e-tourism, all stakeholders should be involved and technology must be updated from time to time to ensure viability. Moreover, encouragement and marketing must be one step forward for development. These actions should be as follows:

- Awareness and productivity assurance from different stakeholders

All stakeholders should be involved in the management of e-tourism. Private and public sector should work together to achieve higher development in this field. All companies should encourage each other to move toward ICT to improve their work and increase their customer satisfaction. Moreover, the local people should know what is e-tourism and how to deal with it, if they are not interested, then it won't succeed.

- Quality standards assurance

It is highly important to have standards to work on. No planning can be done without putting the steps for development. These steps are the standards that companies should be committed to in managing e-tourism.

- Set regulations and legislations and policy making

Setting the rules in a framework to work on is part of building a plan. To achieve it, the government should make some actions in this regard. In Lebanon, still no policies are considered to improve or at least be aware of such type of tourism that has been spreading all over the world in such a small time that even few countries are following this update.

- ICT development

Developing technologies that can lead to e-business is not an easy way. However, Lebanese people are smart; they have the power to develop anything if they had the money. The only thing that is needed is the help of the NGOs and private partners to manage and maintain technology development in the country.

- Regional partnerships

There is huge need to ensure work between Lebanon and its neighbors. UAE is working on such development, so there should be strategies to work together to ensure cooperation and development of information technology not only in Lebanon, but also in the Arab countries as a whole.

5.4 Tourism Before the internet

Before the appearance of the internet, tourism was dependent on TAs, TOs, and reservations were made through reservation systems only. Hotels, car rentals companies, and restaurants also included in the Tour operator's job for building a package tour, but they weren't seen or known globally until the beginning of the internet.

5.5 Tourism after the internet

All the tourism and hospitality services that were made manually have taken a shift towards the internet after the development of information technology. Selling has become easier through internet, and contact between consumer and producer is going to vanish after a while, and all the information has become in the customers' hands leading to easiness of work and time consumption has decreased.

5.6 E-tourism Organizational Chart

The chart on the next page shows us how tourism is connected with its companies,, its types and how to pay when doing any action related to tourism reservations . It also summarizes how e-tourism is related to it and that it is a part of e-business, that is divided into e-commerce, e-marketing, and e-tourism. E-tourism is divided into 2 parts which include the internet and the ICT which is information and communication technology.

It is a chart summarizing the tourism industry in global, and e-tourism in specific, and how they are related to each other's.

On the next chapter, it will discuss how to make a tourism website more attractive and interesting so that its users won't get bored easily and leave it quickly.

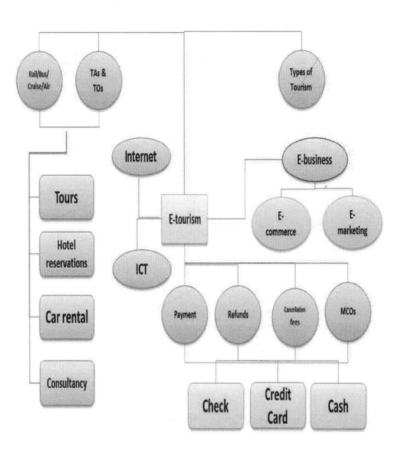

Chapter 6: Online Usage

It is very important to see that websites are as much important in their designs as that in their information that they have. So it is vital to know what are the steps that should be taken into consideration to build an attractive website.

We should bear in mind the reason a customer has when entering a website, there are many, but the most important one is to get knowledge, that's why we should consider developing the website and facilitate customer usability to ensure user-friendly and great experience for the customer.

Many criteria should be taken into consideration:

a. The attractiveness of the website.

It is known that when you enter a website, the first thing that attracts you is the color and shape of the website. If the colors weren't attractive and some harmony exits between them, then the visitor will leave the page immediately.

b. User-friendly website

It is highly recommended to view a website and work on it in an easy way. No need for somebody's help when navigating the website.

c. ensure online trust

The scariest step customers fear of is when they want to purchase a ticket, and they are not sure whether the purchase will be safe or not. So, it is vital to ensure our loyalty to customers as this will increase visitor's trust and build good image for the website.

d. Put "make reservation" on the first page

It is important for the first-time visitors and loyal ones to see when entering the website, the location of where they can make a reservation so that won't take time to search for the location of creating a reservation since as we all know "Time is Money" and people get bored easily nowadays, so we have to offer them full service will less time.

e. Flexibility during reservation

It is good to ensure flexibility during a reservation, like giving the customer the opportunity to see many flights that can be seen during choosing his best choice.

f. Show prices fast

It is highly needed to let customers see the price of the flight before choosing it. When the customer sees the prices of different flights directly without going to many pages to reach his goal, this will help him choose the right flight fast.

Figure 9: The price is directly shown when you just set the time of departure and arrival

g. Calendar

It has been noted that if the calendar exists during making a reservation, it will facilitate the job of the customer to search for the dates that he/she wants and can directly pick the date that are needed just be clicking on the calendar.

Figure 10: The calendar is set on departing and returning in order to set the departing/returning time

h. Offer competing prices

To increase the number of customers, the website should offer prices that can help compete with others in the market. This will not only bring extra customers, but will develop good vision for this website and high preference in using such a website for issuing tickets or accommodation …

i. Show different currency prices

To ensure that you are offering all the information for all types of customers, ensure to have the price in multi-currencies. This will ease turning the price from a currency to another and less time usage.

j. Have a map for the offered flights

It is a good idea to show the customer the routing of the flight that he has chosen.

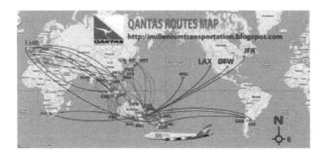

Figure 11: A map showing different route flights for Qantas

k. Ensure safety and security

The highest problem is to break the wall of entrust between the company and the customer. In order to do this, safety and security should be considered and ensured and avoid the concept of being a hacker or stealing website. This could ruin the website in no time.

1. Recommendations

It is very priceless to see what others have left after using a website. It can help new customers to build a view about this website and see whether they will continue surfing it or not. It is part of "word of mouth".

An Example of a good Usable Website

There are many websites that are usable and one of these websites is BOENSO which will be discussed now.

BOENSO Products:

1- Help open up new markets.

2- Help businesses to win more customers.

3- Help increase profits.

4- Ensure highest level of customer satisfaction and service.

5- Enjoy great experience.

6- Up-to-date technologies.

7- Gives 24/7 help for customers.

8- Ensure Professionalism.

9- Ensure best value for money.

10- Directly connected to Airline Booking Systems.

11- Offers qualified programmers with knowledge of C/C++, etc…

12- Only show journeys which are really available and which can be booked directly.

13- Can pay through different payment methods.

14- Extra services can be booked (airline seats, meals…).

15- Can be connected to any e-ticketing system.

16- Are easy to use.

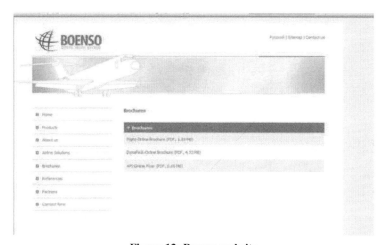

Figure 12: Boenso website

Summary

Finally, we can conclude that if we want to make a website, we should take into account its usability which includes design, security, services offered and everything that can facilitate the customer's resevation process so that they won't get bored during their practices and make their reservations with less time consuming.

On the next chapter, an application was designed, made and developed by me as a virual tour on the underwater tourism in Lebanon by applying them through a website.

Chapter 7: Virtual tour

A virtual tour is a simulation of an existing location, it allows users to view, listen, and sometimes interact with the seen product. It is as if you are at the destination. An example of a good virtual tour is the Louvre museum website, you can see all the artifacts there in each room from your home, there is no need to go and see them live, you can see them from your location.

7.1 History

The beginning of virtual tourism was in 1994, as museum interpretation of Dudley castle in England, designed by Colin Johnson, who is a British engineer, in which Queen Elizabeth II encouraged them type of tour and built a system that describes virtual tour as "Virtual Tour, being a cross between Virtual Reality and Royal Tour".

7.2 Why Virtual Tours

The internet is the primary source for tourism information. There is an increase use of the internet for different services that are related to tourism. So why not to develop virtual tourism, it is one of the most important services offered to customers. It won't stop tourism as many consider, it actually will increase travel since when tourists know about the destination they are interested in, and view it, and they would get more encouraged to go to that destination, not be provoked.

Virtual tour offers experience for website visitors, unlike viewing pictures only, or reading just information.

7.3 Virtual Tourism of "Lebanon Underwater" Through a Website

Website Name: www.lebanonunderwater.webs.com , this website is created by me, and the idea of making an underwater tourism website is Lebanon came from my License project in 2010. (Fig. 32 shows the homepage of this website).

Figure 13: website's homepage

This tourist website is a way to inform its visitors about the underwater ruins in several cities in Lebanon. It is a "web 2" type of websites as it allows visitors to explore and gain information. It also allows them to register (open an account) and insert and discuss their comments, posts and news. For this, it allows visitors integration (without being responded automatically from the website's system". It's published as a free website (Origin: webs.com) in March 2011.

7.4 SWOT Analysis of the website

SWOT analysis is an analysis that is made to obtain strength, weaknesses, opportunities and threats for any project.

7.4.1 Strengths

7.4.1.1 Domain name

The name of the website is created to be flexible and easily accessible in a way:

- It would be broader for more subjects and edited to exceed one country.

- It specifies both words **"LEBANON"** and **"UNDERWATER"** as domain names in order to create an accessible way for websites' visitors in finding this website through searching engines (Google, Wikipedia, YouTube, and yahoo…etc.).

- It would be a good link from further websites (as a marketing tool for the country) and, at the same time, it is a good access for related links.

7.4.1.2 Personality of the website

- The dominated color of the website (Water Blue) is chosen since it is also the color of sea that reflects the type of tourism we are discussing in it

- Familiarity of the website: It is familiar and clear for all visitors when using the website through its navigating keys (some are mentioned previously).

- The logo used for this website:

- It is localized correctly at the upper of the home page, as the website is English oriented.

- It is chosen to be The Sea photo which is the basic part of this website.

7.4.1.3 Distributing Channels

- Links are mentioned in a separate section. They lead to some websites that are related to virtual or e-tourism.

- But, these websites don't link it back for marketing requirements (This is a weak point that will be mentioned in weaknesses section).

- Sending messages to the members and "contact us" section is also considered as a fine distributing channel.

- Other distributing channels like "Facebook" and "twitter"…etc.

7.4.1.4 Visitors' Integration

This website also allows visitors to register, then, post their "news" and comment on all photos/videos. It also allows them to add photos/videos

7.4.2 Weaknesses

7.4.2.1 Marketing process

This website is not marketed yet as a link from other websites (Distributing channels), neither through pop up advertisements in other websites.

In addition, No, "set as my favorite page" or "forward to a friend" options are available yet.

7.4.2.2 Videos, photos and text

- Long paragraphs and not short sentences exit. But, in this website, it is not considered to be as a weak point, since it targets researchers who need information about this type of tourism to get extra information of what they are looking for.

7.4.3 Opportunities

The opportunities that would be exploited to improve this website are to market and update it as follows:

- New related links that would link back the website.

- New events that would also be updated through administrator and members.

7.4.4 Threats

This website is threaten by copy right. As it is a free website. Moreover, information would undergo "copy-paste" easily.

For this, another way for publishing is preferable and it is through Microsoft Expression Web.

Now, I am going to describe in more details every navigation key.

NAVIGATING KEYS USED IN THE WEBSITE

Blog	Contact Us
Photo Gallery	Calendar
Videos	Useful Links
Members	Arcade
Guest Book	

7.5 Blog

It is a web that contains a person's life and all the information that he has. It is not only data that a person has; it is also used for publishing and sometimes interacting.

Blogs are called weblogs. They are important that summarize the information and help to analyze the person you are searching for by viewing his blog. Blogs can be used for building e-portfolios that include CVs, person's achievements, certificates he obtained… it is a new way for developing person's data by creating a blog.

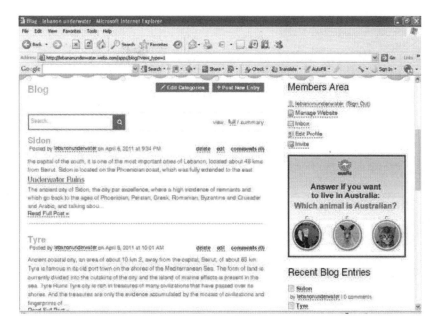

Figure 14: In the blog page, I put all the information about Tyre and Sidon's underwater ruins

In my website, the Blog includes information about Tyre and Sidon, their history and their attractions that are underwater. Visitors can comment on the information and they also can post more information if they like. The Blog is also the home page of the website.

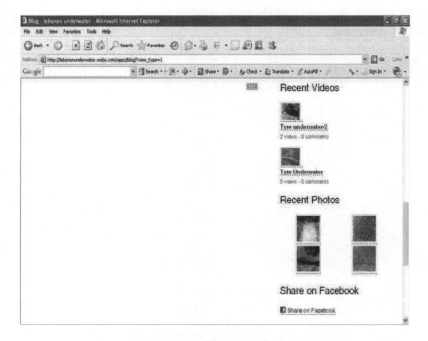

Figure 15: Also photos and videos can be entered from here

Here, we are still on the same website and from it we can go to either the videos or photos or even the games. As we can also see, on this page, we can share all the information on Facebook by just clicking on "share on Facebook".

7.6 Photo Gallery

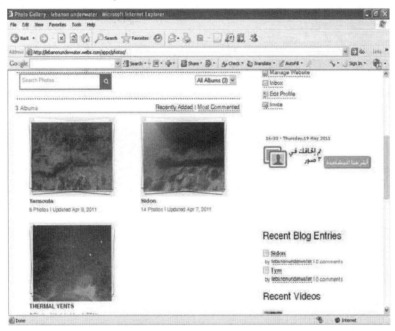

Figure 16: 3 albums are available

Here, 3 Photo Albums are inserted, one for Thermal vents (which are in Tyre), one for Sidon, and one for Yarmouta. Every album includes several photos about the attractions in each country.

7.7 Videos

Figure 17: 2 Videos about Tyre ruins are available

Until now, 2 videos have been downloaded, both would allow the visitor to see the underwater ruins in Tyre, and also they can post their comments about them in a very easy way.

7.8 Calendar

Figure 18: here is the calendar

Calendar of events that will be always updated when some events might get applicable for any future events that could be done from diving, 3-D Video playing about the underwater attractions, to making parties and maybe some festivals around the attraction location as a marketing tool.

7.9 Useful Links

Figure 19: many links related to tourism, ruins underwater and diving in Lebanon are now applied at my website

Many links are inserted until now. One of these links are the ministry of tourism link, scuba diving Lebanese website, Lebanese travel guide and a lot more that can be helpful for such type of tourism.

7.10 Arcade

Arcade includes 5 games so that whenever the customer feels bored, he can play one of these games and then return to the main website information.

7.11 Members

Members include all the people that have joined the website and interfered in it in some way.

7.12 Guest Book

Here if the customer wants to leave a comment, he can mail it to me and I will reply him for any information he would like to have.

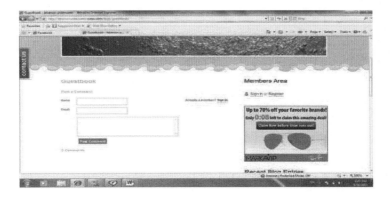

Figure 20: the Guest book page

7.13 Contact Us

If the customer needs some extra information about this type of tourism, or some problems that is facing him in the website, he can contact me through the navigation button "Contact Us".

7.14 Conclusion

Finally, we can say that "Lebanon Underwater" is a fine sample about virtual tourism which is publically marketed and distributed through a website that deals with e-tourism. Following the best standards that a website is preferred to include, www.lebanonunderwater.webs.com has been undergone a slight reassessment in order to improve the strong points, overcome the week points, catch the opportunities and be careful of the threats.

In the next chapter, e-tourism is subjected through its marketing. Many ways to market e-tourism are found and explained in details in chapter 8, so have a look if you are interested.

Chapter 8: Marketing

Marketing has become a driving force in modern global economy and a key element that helps attaining our goals.

For developing marketing strategy, it is important to make research on what customers want, and know their needs in order to build the product design and build a promotion plan.

How to market websites?

It is important to develop good website and inform customers about its existence. This can be done through emails and word of mouth.

Internet marketing is expensive, yet there can be ways to promote a website by simple steps.

After analyzing Lebanon's potential for the e-commerce market, it is clear that Lebanon has a lot to offer and to do. But are we aware of these huge chances? I think promotion is the only solution to be more present.

Before demonstrating the promotion tools, we should mention Philip Kotler's 4 Ps that constitute the marketing mix. These are: product, price, place and promotion.

8.1 Marketing Mix (by Philip Kotler)

8.1.1 Product

8.1.1.1The core product

The core product is the basic product that customers request and are in need for.

Internet offers value for the service any customer requests. We can consider a virtual tour as a core product of the tourism service for example.

8.1.1.2 The extended Product

It is the additional benefits after obtaining the basic needs which is the core product. One of these extended products are customer feedback, money-back offers, customer services, etc…

8.1.2 Price

Price offerings through the internet are highly competitive yet always changing. There is no base for prices given on the internet.

This can increase competition. Lebanese travel agencies enjoy lower margin of prices and processes. Nowadays, there is negotiation, counter trade, strategic alliances, technology transfer, leasing as well as auctions.

Prices are complex, and options for the price tourism packages include:

- Basic price.

- Refund policies.

- Discounts.

- Miscellaneous requests.

8.1.3 Place

The place involves the place of purchase, distribution, and consumption.

For e-tourism, place won't be a problem, whether online or not, the product will be received to the consumer anywhere, any time.

8.1.4 Promotion

Promotion is how to reach largest number of people through using different communication tools.

These communication tools can be through advertising, public relations, e-mails, word of mouth, etc... all these can be done online in which will promote tourism by using ICT.

In case of promoting e-tourism in Lebanon, promotion is to reach all locals and foreigners and develop Lebanese travel agencies.

8.2 E-tourism marketing in Lebanon

Developing e-tourism will be through e-commerce. It can be done through 4 steps which are:

1.   Ensuring the availability of developed servers so that internet will be available and developed more effectively on the ground.

2.   Ensure funding with the help of private and public sector. This will ensure cooperation of both sectors and development of online tourism.

3.   Develop different types of media and ensure high quality staff for achieving good promotion and marketing for e-tourism.

4.   Build legislations and regulations for achieving the 3 steps above. The Lebanese government must work on building new policy rules, related to tourism in general, and e-tourism in specific to ensure a successful tourism industry, and as we know, Lebanon is based for its

economy on tourism only, so to develop tourism we should start in its basic foundation steps and building regulations is one of these steps.

8.3 Global Audience

Websites have increased open-information for all consumers around the world. So, it is very effective to let the global know about what Lebanon has to offer in tourism-related products.

Travel agencies in Lebanon should encourage customers to use online services rather than using voice contact to the call center. Usually if the customer use the "contact us", then it will reduce the needs of contact the center and it make it available 24 hours for the customer.

8.4 Promoting the Website

Most of the Lebanese travel agencies have a website, but in order to enter more in the market and receive more customers they need to promote their websites. This can be by using emails, sending messages for different people. Moreover, word of mouth can reach big number of customers. Also, using social media nowadays like Facebook, creating a Facebook page about the company (travel agency, hotel…) will promote it and will reach all people around the world.

After creating a Facebook page, it can reach customers easily through just liking the page that will be seen on all Facebook audience, and then viewing this page and getting information about the company and interacting with it.

There are 2 techniques to drive traffic to the website. These are push and pull techniques that are discussed in the second page.

8.4.1 Pull techniques

Pull techniques are ways to attract visitors to a website.

8.4.1.1 Web directories

A web directory is a directory on the World Wide Web that specializes in linking to other websites and categorizing those links. The first of them was "yahoo".

8.4.1.2 Search engines

Google, Yahoo, Hotmail can be good search engines to be used for promotion.

8.4.1.3 Links

Links helps reaching information easier than ever. Putting keywords help reach the website easier than just publishing the website without having words that summarize the information that the link has.

For example, the text "online e-tourism" with a link to "www.onlineEtourism.com" is better than the link alone. If travel agencies want the site to be listed in the search engines, the keyword "E-tourism".

8.4.1.4 Contextual Links

For example an advertiser purchases the word "Lebanon". If www.cnn.com subscribes to the program, a link to the advertiser's website will be played on the page that deals with Lebanon on Cnn.com.

8.4.2 Push techniques

Push is the set of strategies to push the information towards the user.

8.4.2.1 E-mails

An electronic mail message reaches the customer and delivers the information. It is also an excellent tool for TA that can use to keep customers constantly informed of their new products, special offers and promotions.

8.4.2.2 Blogs

Placing links to the website in blogs that deals with topics related to e-tourism can generate traffic to the website. A blog is a publicity accessible personal journal for an individual. It is similar to a personal diary, but one that is shared over the web.

8.4.2.3 Word of Mouth

The most powerful form of promotion is word-of-mouth. They are more likely if the website has a clear and useful function and works well. If it is good so the people will recommend it to others. Also, if the company is known, others can reach its website fast through word-of-mouth.

As being said in Chapter 2, Tripadvisor is successful because of the reviews people leave on its website. This affects positively on building trust for consumers for the website in which will increase customers' visit and encourage them to give their own opinions.

If the travel agencies need to encourage people to use more the website they can add a "recommend this web to your friends" button on their website and make it easy for users to forward pages on the site to other people.

8.4.2.5 Public Relations

It is primarily about events and press releases. Public relation, in the context of destination promotion, means working with the media to generate positive publicity and to counter negative publicity about your area while telling the truth.

Travel agencies can generate PR coverage through a success story connected with their website or by offering unusual features on it.

Using press releases has several advantages:

- Travel agencies can generate publicities through Lebanese press releases launched on the internet like: Al-Balad…

- Launching a free e-mail newsletter.

- Launching new services on your site such as introduction to online booking.

-New customers or success stories resulting from launch/ development of your site

-Changes and improvements to your site.

8.5 Training

Staffs are the major source for developing good marketing. They should be motivated to achieve high company goals. After ensuring their motivation, they should be trained.

Travel agencies in Lebanon should do a specific performing program that helps the staff to be able to do online transactions, attend customer emails and calls, and answer frequent asked questions.

As a summary, having a happy staff will lead to happy customers, in which it will generate happy stakeholders.

8.6 Ministry of Tourism

In order to have more awareness of e-tourism in Lebanon, the ministry should:

- Establish a fully operational industry website. This will present relevant information in an accessible form, allowing tourism businesses to improve the nature of the services they provide, and tailor their individual marketing plans to suit particular niche markets.

- With this website, the ministry can establish a partnership with the private sectors in Lebanon to maintain competitive advantages through further development.

- This new website will develop the facility to book and pay by e-commerce for events happening in Lebanon such as "Beiteddine Festival" or "Baalbeck Festival" and let the tourists use the latest technologies such as the provision of information through mobile phone.

- Establish tourist information and booking center that will be available through a single and international telephone number.

- Enhance the niche market strategy by establishing "holiday offices departments" around the world with the help of MEA. This will help tourism companies to cooperate when advertising overseas and assist in the marketing and promotion of e-tourism in Lebanon.

8.7 Interactive Digital Television Distribution (IDTV)

It is mentioned that IDTV based tourism distribution benefits from several factors:

- It enables a more relaxed atmosphere than when using internet.

- It is interactive.

8.8 Online Shopping Security

Thanks to the internet, we can order book, book tickets and hotels online across the ocean. While the internet helps making our life more convenient, it also provides a gateway to our personal information: home, worksite, security..

Ensuring security would build relaxation for the customer and encourage him to buy from this website once, twice, and a lot more.

If proper measures are taken for ensuring security, then online shopping would become very safe. However, it also should be noticed on how to ensure that this website is safe? Just a small talk about the website that it is not safe, can ruin the website's good reputation.

The most important thing is to recognize secure sites and check for lock and key items that appears on the screen.

For example, Gullivers is a company that allows its customers to reserve hotels all over the world online.

It explains its policy on user privacy and data security. The information stored when making a reservation are the name, address, contact telephone number, e-mail address and credit card number of the customer.

Chapter 9: Conclusion

9.1 General impacts

The highly important feature for e-tourism is to build good reputation in order to succeed in the market.

Through this study, we have explored the travel and tourism market and discussed the impact of e-tourism and its effect on tourism as a whole by studying its different perspectives.

Some problems that I have faced during preparing my thesis were lack of contribution from the ministry of tourism and the ministry of telecommunication, especially the second one that I felt were very afraid to give any information about the new development steps that have taken to improve the internet in Lebanon after trying to take an interview with the minister's consultant. Also there were some problems of getting answers from agents related to answering my questions.

The internet is a value that can be offered for its consumers. It gives information, views, online reservations, services, virtual tours and yet more to come.

In Lebanon, E-tourism is becoming more and more developed every day. Most of the Travel agencies and hotels are moving to the electronic reservation with their applicable websites to help their customers attaining their needs through a fast way.

Another idea concluded was the importance of having a usable website through its design, privacy, and its offers to its customer.

Also, many development processes have been discussed to manage and improve e-tourism in chapter 5 which are the purpose of the study.

In the following, I will present the most important ideas, steps, and results that are taken to achieve my project about E-tourism and its revolutionary effect in general.

9.2 Case studies

I studied four cases in order to improve and develop my project, from them many things helped me to find ways to improve e-tourism like taking customer's reviews in a website, putting a strategy for developing e-tourism that can open better future e-tourism in the years coming.

9.3 E-tourism in the Future

E-tourism is the future of the whole tourism industry only if it is taken into account and all the communication and specified technologies were available, then E-tourism will facilitate the life of the future customers.

In Lebanon, after 4 interviews, it turned out that most of reservations are turning now to be accomplished on the internet and most agencies and hotels are referring to their websites to make reservations.

9.4 Statistics

After 2 questionnaires, one distributed on customers and one on travel agencies, the results showed that most customers are turning on making reservations on the internet because it is easier and less time consuming, and about the agencies, most of them are developing their own websites for their customers to help them in their reservations or even helping them with anything they would need through the "contact us".

9.5 Effect of E-tourism

Many advantages might come from e-tourism:

- Fast customer service.

- Better prices offered.

- Customers can make their reservations by their own.

Possible disadvantages have also been identified. These include:

- Misleading information that might confuse tourists.

- Lack of security.

- High competition that might lead to vanish of small enterprises

9.6 Lebanon Underwater Website

I have made a website about underwater tourism in Lebanon. This website was undergone a SWOT analysis study to discuss all its positive and negative points and it shows all ruins underwater.

9.7 Management of E-tourism

Several steps to manage and improve e-tourism have been listed and discussed so that to make e-tourism more developed and improved for the next generation.

9.8 Marketing

To promote a website, through pull and push techniques, to put marketing strategy, and with the help of ministry of tourism and using newest technologies, marketing this type of tourism can be accomplished with the best ways.

9.9 Last words

Finally, I will conclude my thesis by these last words:

The thesis title is still going under many discussions and research, so it won't be closed for a long time from now since internet is the technology of the future, so what will be its destiny? And how would it change the life of people?? Well, only time will show us and hopefully someone will continue where I have stopped in this thesis.

Table of Figures

References

- Duff, A., 2002,*E-tourism in England-A strategy for modernizing English tourism through e-business*. Also Available From:

  http://www.insights.org.uk/articleitem.aspx?title=E-Tourism+in+England

  [Cited on 3 February 2011]

- E-tourism at a glance…..Vietnam, Available from:

  http://www.unctadxi.org/sections/SITE/etourism/docs/Vietnam.pdf

  [Cited on 5 February 2011]

- Sheldon, P. 1993, Destination information systems. Annals of Tourism Research, 20 (4).

- Gretzel, U., 2007, *Online Travel Review Study-Role and Impact of online travel reviews*, available also at :http://www.tripadvisor.com/pdfs/OnlineTravelReviewReport.pdf

- Buhalis, D. 2003, *E-Tourism: Information Technology for Strategic Tourism Management*. London, UK: Pearson (Financial Times/Prentice Hall).

- Hoffman, D., 2000, *The revolution will not be televised: Introduction to the special issue on Marketing Science and the Internet. Marketing Science*.

- Dutton, W. H., and Helsper, E. J. (2007). Oxford Internet survey 2007 report: The Internet in Britain. Oxford, UK: Oxford Internet Institute, University of Oxford. Available from:

http://www.oii.ox.ac.uk/research/oxis/OxIS2007_Report.pdf.

[Cited on 12 February 2011]

- Buhalis, 2004, *eAirlines: strategic and tactical use of ICTs in the airline industry-information and management.*

- Omni Tourism, Architects of E-tourism Marketing and Technology, Available From:

  http://www.omnitourism.com/

  [Cited on 8 February 2011]

- Turban et al, 2008, *Electronic commerce 2008: A managerial perspective, upper saddle river*, Pearson education,Inc.

- Figures published by VisitScotland (2002) in Tourism in Scotland 2001).

- Virtual Tour. Available from:
http://en.wikipedia.org/wiki/Virtual_tour

  [Cited on 8 August 2011]

- Egger, R., and Buhalis, D.,2008. *eTourism Case Studies: Management and Marketing Issues*, Burlington, MA: Elsevier.

- Practical ecommerce, basic definitions: web1.0,web 2.0, web3.0. Available from:

http://www.practicalecommerce.com/articles/464-Basic-Definitions-Web-1-0-Web-2-0-Web-3-0

[Cited on 7 March 2011]

- Buhalis, D., and Law, R. 2008. Progress in information technology and tourism management: 20 years on and 10 years after the Internet – The state of eTourism research, Tourism Management, 29 (4).

- Web 1.0, Web 2.0 and Web 3.0 Simplified for Nonprofits. Available from:

http://nonprofitorgs.wordpress.com/2010/01/28/web-1-0-web-2-0-and-web-3-0-simplified-for-nonprofits/

[Cited on 7 March 2011]

- Buhalis, D., and Zoge, M. ,2007, *The strategic impact of the Internet on the tourism industry. In M. Sigala, L. Mich, & J. Murphy (Eds.). Information and Communications Technologies in Tourism: Proceedings of the International Conference ENTER in Ljubljana,* Slovenia. Springer-Verlag Wien (ISBN: 978-3-211-69564-7).

- Buhalis, D., and Licata, C. ,2002. *The e-tourism intermediaries. Tourism Management*, 23 (3).

- Gupta, U., 2000,*Information Systems: Success in the 21st Century*, Upper Saddle River, NJ: Prentice Hall.

- Porter, M. ,2001,*Strategy and the Internet*, Harvard Business Review, 103D (March).

- Rayman-Bacchus, L. and Molina, A., 2001, Internet-based tourism services: business issues and trends in Futures, 33.

- Gratzer, M., *A framework for Competitive Advantage in eTourism*, Vienna.

- Buhalis, D., Jun, S.,2011, *E-tourism – CTR*.

- The Scottish parliament, the information center, 2002, Tourism E-business, Scotland.

- ورداني,يوسف 2008, كيفية تنظيم السياحة الالكترونية و مردودها على صناعة السياحة, مصر,

- رشا علي الدين أحمد, السياحة الالكترونية حلم دبى القادم نظرة قانونية, متوفرة عبر:

Available from:http://www.omn0.net/forum/showthread.php?t=11736

[Cited on 15 May 2011]

- هند محمد حامد, 2003, التجارة الالكترونية في المجال السياحي, القاهرة

[Cited on 15 May 2011]

- Usability ROI Declining, But Still Strong. Available From:www.useit.com/alertbox/20030107.html

[Cited on 17 March 2011]

- L. Chen and T. Justin, 2004, *Technology adaption in e-commerce: Key adoption of online shopping*, Information & Management.

- Online Travel sector usability. Available from:

http://www.webcredible.co.uk/user-friendly-resources/white-papers/online-travel-sector-usability.pdf

[Cited on 5 February 2011]

- Bakos, Y. ,1998, the emerging role of electronic marketplaces on the internet.

- D. Gefen and D. W. Straub, 2004, *Consumer trust in B2C e-commerce and the importance of socialpresence: experiments in e-products and e-services*, Omeg.

- Hitwise UK, Online search report 2005. Available From:

http://www.sempo.org/resource/resmgr/Docs/HitwiseUKSearchReport.pdf

[Cited on 8 August 2011]

- YouGov survey of 1,955 people (May 2005)

- 2005/6 Barclaycard Business Travel Survey .Available From: www.companybarclaycard.co.uk/information_centre/tibs/tibs2005_06_survey.pdf

[Cited on 25 March 2011]

- ABTA (November 2005), Available from: http://www.webcredible.co.uk/user-friendly-resources/white-papers/online-travel-sector-usability.pdf

[Cited on 15 February 2011]

- M. Cao, Q. Zhang, and S. J., 2005, *B2C e-commerce web site quality: an empirical examination*, Industrial Management & Data Systems.

- R. Kalakota and A. B. Whinston, 1997,*Electronic Commerce: A Manager's Guide*. Addison Wesley.

- BOENSO… Available from: http://www.boenso.net/en/about-us/-

[Cited on 5 February 2011]

- Susan S. Lukesh ,1995,CSA Newsletter, Imaging The Past,Vol. VII, No. 4

- Virtual Tours of Dudley Castle archive, Available From:http://www.exrenda.net/dudley/index.htm

[Cited on 6 February 2011]

- Imaging the Past' - *Electronic Imaging and Computer Graphics in Museums and Archaeology* - ISBN 0-86159-114-3

-Weblog.Available from

http://www.marketingterms.com/dictionary/blog/

[Cited on 8 August 2011]

- kotler, P.,2002,*Marketing , an introduction,* sixth edition.

-Core Product, Available from: http://www.businessdictionary.com/definition/core-product.html

[Cited on 16 September 2011]

-Globalization. Available from:

http://en.wikipedia.org/wiki/Globalization

[Cited on 16 September 2011].

Appendices

Appendix A
<u>Questionnaire 1</u>

This questionnaire is made for a thesis of title: "E-tourism Revolutionary Effect". In order to see where Electronic tourism has reached and to know whether customers are interested in booking online and getting information about travel trips and attractions, this questionnaire would be very helpful.

Sex:...

Age:...

- Do you know about E-tourism?

    - yes.

    - no.

- electronic tourism is how to book and how to get information about the place you are going to. Now, have you ever used any website related to reservations and booking?

- Yes.

- No.

- If yes, how many times have you done it?

- Every time I want a reservation.

- Only when I am in a hurry.

- When I find that they are less costly than booking at an agency.

- Why do you use the internet rather than going to an agency or tour operator?

- Gaining extra time/faster service.

- Less costly.

- Others, please specify:...

- What services related to your trip do you purchase online?

- Car rental.

- Room reservation.

- Tour booking.

- Restaurant reservation.

- Would E-tourism in Lebanon increases tourism cash flow?

- It won't affect tourism at all.

- Moderately increases tourism flow.

- Highly increases tourism flow.

- Do you think that the ministry of tourism should promote E-tourism in Lebanon?

- Yes.

- Maybe.

- No.

- Do you think that the private sector should promote e-tourism in Lebanon?

- Yes

- Maybe

- No

- What are the ways for promoting E-tourism in Lebanon?

- Through T.V, facebookadvertising,.......

- Through ambassadors

- With the contribution of travel agencies, hotels, car rentals, etc.

- Others:...

- Do you think that the ministry of telecommunication in Lebanon would affect on E-tourism?

- Yes

- No

  If yes, how??

- What do you think about the product you are getting from the internet would be?

- Virtual.

- Information-rich product.

- Opportunity to buy last minute.

- Open all hours.

- Reduced costs (discounts, promotions…)

- More than an option for any type of reservation.

- Finally, do you think that E-tourism would succeed in Lebanon?

- Definitely.

- Maybe.

- No.

Why?

....

....

Appendix B

Questions distributed on TAs are:

1) Do you have a website?

2) Why?

3) Has it brought extra revenues?

4) What are its negative impacts?

5) Are you using a CRS or the internet only for reservations?

6) Do you have employees following your reservations on the internet?

Abbreviations

- GDS: Global distribution system
- CRS: Central reservation system
- DMC: Destination Management Company
- DMO: Destination Marketing Organization.

- DES: Destination Enterprise System

- ICT: information communication technology.

- SWOT: Strength,weakness,opportunity,threat.

- ETC: electronic tourism and communication.

- WTO: World Tourism Organization.

- TITC: Technology and Information Tourism Center.

- ISP: Internet Server Provider.

- UNCTAD: UN conference on trade and development

- TA: Travel agency.

- TO: Tour Operator.

- EITO: European Information Technology Observatory.

- ONS: Office of National Statistics.

- IT: Information Technology.

- BTA: Business Technology Association.

- SME: Small and Medium Enterprise

- CRM: Customer Relationship Management.

- FAQ: Frequently Asked Questions

- BOENSO: Booking Engine Software.

- API: Application Programming Interface.

Index

Druck: KN Digital Printforce GmbH · Schockenriedstraße 37 · 70565 Stuttgart